Musings on
LEADERSHIP

Life lessons to help you thrive as a leader

Tor Mesoy et al.

Agnus
Consulting
Investing in people

Published by Agnus Consulting
© 2019 Agnus Consulting Ltd. All rights reserved
ISBN: 978-988-79698-0-8

Printed in Hong Kong, China

About this anthology

Why this anthology?

We have worked on the topics of leadership and leadership development for decades now. The field is vast, and I know that complete
mastery is an ideal rather than something that can be fully achieved.
Every day brings something new. Every leader we work with is
unique, and grapples with particular challenges and opportunities.
How do we make sense of the richness of these diverse experiences?
One way is to write. Writing can help us process experiences and it
can bring clarity. Over the years, we have regularly written on topics
associated with leadership – be it leading yourself, leading your teams
or leading others where you have no formal authority. Now felt like
the right time to collect some of what we have written, and assemble
an anthology. We have given this collection the humble title, *Musings
on Leadership*. In it, you will find personal experiences and reflections
– rather than monumental new theories. The musings invite you to
ponder and reflect on your own experiences. We hope that once in a
while you will nod in recognition, or even smile. Once in a while you
may balk and want to challenge us. Do. We welcome your reactions!
Should you wish to get in touch after reading this, please visit our
web site www.agnusconsulting.hk.

Who is this for?

The anthology is for anyone who is open to spending a quiet hour or
so reflecting on leadership and its many facets. The Musings are short

– typically 2-3 pages, so you can easily pick this up and grab a 'snack' during your daily commute.

How was it developed?

As so much of the work we do, the effort to write this anthology was collaborative. We invited a handful of our close associates to contribute their Musings. Thanks to all contributors who believed in the concept and shared their submissions.

Enjoy the read!

Tor Mesoy

Contents

Acknowledgements

As we work with our clients to strengthen leadership in organizations around the world, we also keep learning. Every encounter is a chance to discover something, to see things from a new angle.

We therefore want to acknowledge all the top teams, all our program participants and all our coaching clients who have shared their stories and ideas, asked good questions, and challenged us. Thank you. A particular word of appreciation goes to our clients who have given us permission to share stories from the journeys we have undertaken together.

We also enjoy working with a global network of expert practitioners. Many of them are self-employed, some work in small teams, some in large corporations, others again in academic institutions or think tanks or foundations. Regardless of such technicalities, we regularly band together to give the participants who are here, now, the greatest, most eye-opening, most life-giving experience we can provide. In doing so, we also learn from one another. This network of people is so large that we cannot mention everyone by name. Still, a few of them stand out and deserve to be mentioned.

We want to acknowledge: Warren Ang, Trond Åsdam, Rajiv Ball, Ken Brown, Nick Chatrath, Wendy Chua, Janelle Diller, Chris Dorian, Paul Gentle, Tomas Gustafsson, Glenn Kiser, Betina Koski, Florian Pollner, Tom Revington, Trond Riiber Knudsen, Tom O'Brien, Michael Shamos, Linda Simmons, Lei Sun, Cameron Smoak, Noel Sy-Quia, Nicolai Tillisch, Phil Whitehurst, Brian Woof and Tim Zak.

Chapter 1
Glimpses of leadership

" Ultimately, a leader is not judged so much by how well he or she leads, but by how well he or she serves."

— Kevin Cashman

Learning from the close encounter with an impressive tiger shark – five critical aspects of leadership

Tor Mesoy, Fiji

Inspiring leadership examples are all around us. I recently had the chance to observe leadership in the face of danger and risk in a slightly unusual setting – the close encounter with a 4.8-meter-long tiger shark at 25 meters' depth off the island of Beqa, in Fiji.

The encounter was exhilarating. On earlier dives during the preceding week, we had observed a number of sharks of different species, including white-tips, nurse sharks and bull sharks. We were certainly alert – and the adrenaline was flowing freely – when a group of six bull sharks came to within five meters of us. Sharks normally don't attack humans, of course, but bull sharks are certainly capable of severing a limb, and there have been a number of fatalities.

On this particular dive, the lone tiger shark came in while we were descending, and continued to circle us for 20 minutes. We descended to the bottom and placed ourselves with our backs to a coral wall in order to have some sense of where the shark was coming from. It seemed intensely inquisitive. I am no expert in shark psychology – and I was curious about the shark's intent. Was it just inquisitive or did it also feel threatened? Or hungry? Might it attack? It certainly seemed useful to stay alert. Stefano, the marine biologist who led this dive, had recommended that we always keep eye contact with the shark. It was daunting to look into the eyes of this agile, elegant animal as it approached ... especially at the point when it came straight at me and brushed past me within easy touching distance. I had to crouch on the bottom to avoid the shark bumping into me. This is not common shark behavior. It felt a bit too intimate and after just over 20 minutes, we surfaced. We had collected a truly memorable experience and the saying "quit while you're ahead" seemed to apply.

So ... that was fun. But there is a deeper leadership lesson here. What were the actions that Stefano performed that helped ensure a successful dive for our team? There was real risk involved here. How did he orchestrate the behavior of a group of seven people that he has just met – some of whom had not encountered a shark before and who might freak out? As I reflect on the experience, five critical aspects stand out:

1: Prepare
2: Cast vision

3: Script the critical moves
4: Be supportive
5: Move fast

1: Prepare

Stefano had spent more than a decade in preparation: getting his formal education in marine biology and performing over a thousand dives in diverse conditions. In a relaxed manner, he shared this preparation so that the entire group rapidly gained confidence in his capabilities. Credibility always makes it easier to lead.

2: Cast vision

During the dive briefing, Stefano prepared us thoroughly. He spoke openly about the dangers and the risks, but he also shared why he respects and admires the sharks and why it might be meaningful to seek a close encounter with them. His love of what he is doing and his passion for sharks were contagious.

3: Script the critical moves

Beyond casting vision, Stefano gave specific, detailed instructions. "Keep eye contact with the sharks. Don't touch them. Check your air frequently, as air consumption can rise markedly when you are under stress. Stay close together to avoid having the shark swim between two divers. Let me know if you want to abort your dive, and we will get you to the surface again". These specific instructions helped focus our attention so that there was not too much idle mental capacity to spend on the question of what might go wrong.

4: Be supportive

Stefano led from the front. When the tiger shark got a bit too friendly, he intervened and pushed the shark away. It was clear that Stefano was prepared to accept personal risk if this was required to keep his team safe. His more exposed position made the rest of us trust that we were (probably) OK.

5: Move fast

By turning preparations into a well-orchestrated drill, Stefano left little time for doubt and speculation. As soon as our boat was in position, he asked us to move fast. Don gear. Gather in the water at the surface. Descend together to maximal depth as rapidly as equalization would permit. This left little time for doubt, speculation, and second thoughts about seeking this encounter. The well-rehearsed drill focused our attention and strengthened our confidence that Stefano knew exactly what he was going.

Inspiring leadership examples are all around us. These five aspects are applicable to other challenging situations that require clear leadership, be they personal or organizational. I'll be inspired by this experience for a long time.

Exerting power without formal authority
– The King's Choice

Tor Mesoy, Norway

I often see the idea of leadership equated with the exercise of power, where there is formal authority. Perhaps though, in totality, there is greater impact from the leadership that is exercised *without* formal authority. This is a form of leadership that each one of us can exercise – in our families, in our communities and in our workplaces. For these reasons, I am intrigued by leadership without formal authority and I often find it hugely inspiring.

I recently enjoyed watching the film *The King's Choice*, in Norwegian *Kongens nei* (The King's "no"), directed by Erik Poppe. This historical drama describes the German invasion of Norway in the early days of World War II. It was a special privilege to watch the film with my father, who is in his eighties and who lived through the War and remembers it vividly. The story told in the film is well known to many Norwegians, but perhaps less well known outside the country.

Synopsis: After the British forces lay mines in Norwegian fjords, Germany invades Norway in a bid to control the North Atlantic and protect the transportation of iron ore, which is shipped out through Narvik, in northern Norway, and bound for the German factories. Germany does not declare war on Norway but presents the action as a bid to 'protect Norway and Norwegians from the British hostile forces'. In spite of this friendly cover, Norway perceives the German invasion as an attack, and fires torpedoes and shells at the German war ships as they cruise up the Oslo fjord – at night, with extinguished lanterns and without prior warning. Mobilization in Norway is shambolic, but the King and the Government flee the capital on a train that leaves Oslo a few hours after the skirmishes in the Oslo fjord. All major Norwegian towns are rapidly captured by the Germans, but the King and the Government remain at large, spending nights in private accommodation and driving in private cars by day. The German diplomatic representative in Norway seeks to negotiate, to avoid the loss of life, but the 'negotiations' consist of a thinly veiled ultimatum from Germany – presented to the King personally. The King is clear: Norway is a democracy, and he will take no such decision on his own. He will submit the question to the Government, even though he considers the government to be weak and pliant, and in spite of his fears that the Government has very limited will to stand up to the occupation force. This is the backdrop to the highlight of the film, a stirring scene where the King presents his position to the Government. His stance is clear: he respects the Government's right to make the decision. At the same time, his personal perspective is values-based: if the Government chooses to accept the German ultimatum, he will be forced to abdicate, together with his house (extended family and lineage). This short, poignant speech shames the Government into rejecting the German advance, and Norway is at war. The King is acutely aware that his actions will lead to casualties on both sides, but accepts this responsibility in the context of the greater good that he stands for.

In many conversations about leadership in the organizations I serve, we explore self-leadership and leadership of direct and indirect reports. Just as important, often, is leadership without formal authority. King Haakon VII's speech is an inspiring example of strong leadership that draws more on moral suasion than on formal power. As King, he is a representative for the people and the nation, but his formal power is limited. The King fully understands the power of symbols, though, and uses this understanding to great effect.

He shows due respect for the Government and clearly indicates that he understands other priorities and competing perspectives, including the desire to avoid conflict and save lives. This is a prerequisite for reaching the senior politicians to whom he is speaking. He is somber and terse – conveying in body language and in tone of voice, in pace and in tenor, a message that is entirely consistent with his words. He clearly demonstrates that he is prepared to risk and sacrifice the monarchy in order to stay true to his values and maintain integrity, in keeping with his personal motto: "All for Norway".

I am regularly inspired to see politicians, NGO leaders, church leaders and business leaders risk their own position, the prospect of re-election, their financial safety, and their prestige to advance the cause they are fighting for – with a visceral understanding that they are living for something greater than themselves. A friend of mine rejected a corporate career to start a think tank that would stimulate and nurture a more strategic and positive dialogue about the future of his country. A politician that I know was among the first in the world to advocate a ban on smoking in public places, at a time when this proposal was hugely unpopular and was met with derisory comments from restaurant owners, conference center managers and most voters. This politician was driven by a deep conviction that he was fighting for better health for the entire population. A business leader, who is also a friend, placed his personal prestige and career on the line as he spoke up against objectionable business practices in his own organization. He ended up leaving the organization because of this.

Are you clear that you are living for something greater than yourself? What consequences is this having in your life? Are the people you lead, with or without formal authority, visibly inspired by your vision? What are your moments of powerful leadership when you choose to stand on principle, perhaps at significant personal risk?

Chapter 2
Leading ourselves

*" The key to growth is the introduction
of higher dimensions of consciousness."*

— Lao Tzu

Learning to lead yourself – a lifelong journey

Tor Mesoy, Austria

"Between stimulus and response there is a space. In that space is our power to choose our response. In our response lies our growth and our freedom." — Viktor E. Frankl

I recently found myself worn down and irritated. I was short on sleep. I had just flown to a new time zone. I had a cold and I was running a rather high fever. I had just completed three long, intense work days. And here I was, in the early morning, wishing to check out of my hotel to get to my first meeting of the day ... and there was no one at reception. When the clerk finally arrived, I was not particularly friendly. I wasn't rude, but I was short and perhaps a bit snide. Not proud of it. Not proud at all, and it is mildly embarrassing to share this in public.

Why did I react that way? Or – slightly different question – why did I act that way? Some empathetic readers might say "it is only natural", but that is weak consolation. That which is "natural" is often not so inspiring. This is not the way I wish to be. I know that I am not alone here. And it is not a new problem – it cannot, for example, be put down to jet lag. The Apostle Paul says: "For I do not do the good I want to do, but the evil I do not want to do—this I keep on doing." (Letter to the Romans, 7:19). And Paul was not an evil man. He lived for others and performed great sacrifices.

Long before Paul, Confucius emphasized that leading others starts with leading oneself: "If you yourself are correct, even without the issuing of orders, things will get done; if you yourself are incorrect, although orders are issued, they will not be obeyed" (Huang 134)". Confucius highlighted the duties of a leader by explaining the proper way to think, act, and make decisions in government positions. Qualities such as continual learning, frugality, humility, confidence, commitment, and loyalty are all examples found within his teachings that provide a framework for leadership. And note that these quali- ties - continual learning, frugality, humility, confidence, commitment, and loyalty – are primarily about self-leadership.

I have just been re-reading Viktor E. Frankl's *Man's Search for Meaning*. This book sets a very high bar for self-leadership. It conveys the reflections of an Austrian psychiatrist who was interned in a series of four concentration camps during World War II and survived to tell the story – in spite of odds of surviving that were only 1:28. In his book he shares impressions of daily life, while emphasizing the psychological aspects of living in concentration camps with people dying around him every day.

Re-reading the book left me inspired, humbled and strongly motivated to double my efforts to deepen self-awareness and strengthen self-leadership.

We should probably all (re-) read Frankl's book every couple of years. I used my pen and annotated my copy heavily while reading. Let me share a couple of passages that struck me.

"The attempt to develop a sense of humor and to see things in a humorous light is some kind of trick learned while mastering the art of living. Yet it is possible to practice the art of living even in a concentration camp, although suffering is omnipresent."

"[...] do the prisoners' reactions to the singular world of the concentration camp prove that man cannot escape the influences of his surroundings? Does man have no choice of action in the face of such circumstances? [...] The experiences of camp life show that man does have a choice of action. There were enough examples, often of a heroic nature, which proved that apathy could be overcome, irritability suppressed."

In this light, my less-than-inspiring behavior with the hotel clerk is embarrassing. The combination of jetlag, mild sleep deprivation and fever becomes nothing when held up against the suffering in the concentration camp. So, it is clear that I still have a lot of work to do on self-awareness and self-leadership. Most of us do.

That makes it very meaningful to explore the topics of self-awareness and self-leadership. In this context, we are all learners. Our key role as leaders is not to "teach" but to create a safe arena, hold the space, role-model vulnerability, invite reflection, ask insightful questions, encourage exploration, and celebrate sharing. Perhaps once in a while we can share an authentic example from our own journey.

Leadership of others starts with self-leadership. And achieving inspiring self-leadership is a life-long journey. Let us therefore encourage and support one another as we pursue the quest. And let us celebrate together when we make progress. During the next leg of your journey you could do worse than (re-)read Frankl's book.

Fueling your leadership journey

Warren Ang, Hong Kong

2018 hit me with this reality: no matter what your intentions and values might be, if you're stressed and burnt out, you're going to be a bad leader. You can't give what you don't have, and if you aren't taking care of yourself, you have little chance of being able to be there for others and for those you lead.

Stress and fatigue bring out the shadow side of our top strengths. At my best, I excel at casting vision, crafting strategy and unleashing the full potential of others. At my worst I can just as easily be critical, judgmental, impatient, and unable to bring others along for the ride. I am not the only one.

The answer people often give to the problem of stress and fatigue is to "improve your work-life balance". However well intentioned that idea may be, I've never found it really helpful for two reasons. First, it implies that work and life are separate and that they should be balanced in some determined proportion. In reality, work and life are too integrated to be treated in balance: I get life out of my work, and I also get drained from my work. I get life out of my relationships and leisure activities, and at times, they also drain me. Second, there's no such thing as a "9 to 5" when you're building, growing and running a company. It's the choice you make when you take on that ambition, and a static balance is simply not realistic.

Instead, what I have found helpful is to reframe the concept of work-life balance to the challenge of ensuring you have enough fuel for your current leadership demands. Here are three practical tips that can help you think about this challenge.

1: Ask: do you have enough fuel to go the distance?

Work-life balance is a static goal, which can never be realistically sustained. In contrast, fueling up is something we have to do regularly and it is dynamic. There are peaks and troughs in both work and life, and we need different types and amounts of fuel to make the journey and avoid running on empty.

There are four types of fuel: physical, mental, emotional, and spiritual. The fuel we need varies from person to person and requires self-awareness. For me, ice-hockey is my physical fuel. It refreshes me and is one of the few forms of exercise that I find life-giving. Reading books on psychology and strategy are my mental fuel. Journaling daily is my emotional fuel – twice a day at least — in the morning and evening — to lay out my thoughts and feelings and to recap the day. Reflecting on dreams and prayer is my spiritual fuel.

It's up to you to commit to taking the time to reflect on the leadership journey you are engaged in, and assess the fuel you will need. This can be done as often as daily. This is a big change in thinking for most of us, who think we'll just take a holiday after the busy season is over. That's not usually sustainable and often leads to an unstable leadership style.

What works for you in each of these four types of fuel? To what extent do you think about the fuel you need for the current season and intentionally fuel-up for the journey? Are you running on empty?

2: Start small, slow and sustainable
The temptation when making any sort of behavior change is to go to extremes and make big changes. That's a good way to fail and get discouraged. There's a lot of wisdom in starting small, slow and building up sustainably. I learned this again recently when I started dieting for the first time this year. I remember being excited to make a step change, and being told by my dietician "That's nice, but that's not sustainable".

Instead, what we did was look at my food preferences, lifestyle, habits and construct a meal plan that was, first and foremost, realistic and feasible. Over time, I began to drop back toward my target weight, losing ~10kg over 4 months. Success in one area often creates positive feedback loops – dieting gave me more energy to read and journal, and helped to build up my ability to 'fuel-up' in other areas in my life.

3: Share openly with those you lead and ask for their support

We often forget that those we lead want to help us lead better. Leadership can feel lonely, and it's important to remember that leadership is two-way. As a leader, you have the privilege of leading others. In return, you are to lead them into their potential and take them on a journey to achieve the vision and mission you are working towards. You can get great insights from your team about what works, and what doesn't. They can give you precious feedback to help calibrate whether you're getting the fuel you need for the task at hand. All you need to do is be intentional, be transparent, and ask for their support.

4: A final note: Let go of "being busy"

Being busy can seem cool in your early career: flying from city to city, running from meeting to meeting, fitting in more than what others thought was possible in your 24/7. To me it seemed like something to be proud of. Unfortunately, for many in today's working world, being busy is still being held up as a symbol of how important you are.

We need to let go of the need to be busy in order to provide inspiring leadership and to grow. Your job as a leader is not to be busy. It's to grow yourself and others into their potential and inspire them toward achieving a vision and mission that's bigger than all of us. You simply can't do that if you're busy all the time. Be conscious of the demands placed on you, fuel-up daily for the journey, start small, slow and sustainable, and ask those you lead for their support.

Mastering time management and
making the most of every minute
– 3 steps to success

Nick Chatrath, Oxford

"What would happen if 80% of your effort was focused on high-results-producing activities? … All it takes is pigheaded discipline and determination." — Chet Holmes

There are two types of people: those who write lists, and those who don't write lists.

Two years ago, I smugly thought that I managed my time very effectively because I wrote lists. Very long lists. And that was my problem — my lists were so long that each time I had a few minutes spare I would cherry pick tasks that were quick, easy, or cried the loudest.

But as Gordon MacDonald puts it, *"Not everything that cries the loudest is the most urgent thing. Just because an email comes in asking again for a meeting next week, doesn't mean you have to answer it now."*

I was regularly falling foul of this. How can we attend to what is truly important, on a daily basis?

I found my answer in Chet Holmes' excellent book, *The Ultimate Sales Machine* and I have regularly been putting it into practice since. Holmes calls his method "the time management secret of billionaires". At its core, it's a quick way to make the right kind of plan for your day that will enable you to focus and release time for other activities.

I will share with you three simple steps that helped me – and may help you – make the most of every minute. Here is the first step:

1: List the six most important things you need to get done the next day, and allocate timings to them. The problem with a long list is that you almost never finish it. But psychologically it is a big boost to finish all six items on your list, and to know that they are the most important items.

So here's the rule as Chet Holmes puts it: *"list the six most important things you need to do and, by hook or by crook, get those six things completed each day".*

My list for today looks like this:
- Write first draft of two blogs
- Speak with Bob about the Organizational Effectiveness project
- Respond to emails about meetings and travel

- Create initial draft of a speech about transformation
- Meet with my publisher
- Meet with the leadership team at one of my clients, a large UK healthcare

Key point: No more than six!

Once you have done this, allocate an amount of time to each task.

Your list might now look something like this:

- Write first draft of two blogs (1.5 hours)
- Speak with Bob about the Organizational Effectiveness project (30 minutes)
- Schedule meetings (30 minutes)
- Create initial draft of speech about transformation (2 hours)
- Meet with my publisher (1hour)
- Meet with the leadership team (1 hour)

Key point: the total time allocated needs to be around 6 hours, not 8-12 hours, because unexpected things usually crop up.

This step was revolutionary in turning my productivity around. But on its own, it is not enough. That's where step 2 comes in:

2: Plan and prioritize the day itself: Chet Holmes says that your plan for the day is "not a general guide to how your day might unfold. It must be specific and have a time slot for absolutely everything".

Continuing the example I used earlier, here is my plan for today:

- 0800-0830: Speak with Bob about the Organizational Effectiveness project
- 0830-1000: Write first draft of two blogs
- 1000-1300: Gym, pilates and lunch
- 1300-1330: Schedule meetings

- 1330-1530: Create initial draft of my speech about transformation
- 1530-1600: Buffer period (emails, ad hoc meetings)
- 1600-1700: Meet with my publisher
- 1700-1930: Buffer period
- 1930-2100: Meet with the leadership team

Key point: use buffer periods. These are absolutely essential, because in their absence you risk being constantly derailed by the unexpected. As part of this second step, it is vital to prioritize. Where have you put the most difficult tasks? Many people put them at the end of the day, but typically we have less time and energy at that point in the day.

Key point: Put the most important task first. I love the sense of achievement I get at 10am when I know I have ticked off the single most important (and usually also the hardest) task of the day; it is all plain sailing from there!

Having the list really empowers me to say no to opportunities that come up in the day but do not serve my priorities and what is most important to me.

But that doesn't mean I've become inflexible. My list often won't take up the whole day, but I know at a glance what will make the biggest difference to my wife, my daughters, my neighborhood and my business.

3: Focus on preparing your time plan daily and on doing one thing at a time. If you want to make the most of every minute, then invest 15 minutes per day in planning your use of time. See below how this works.

- Put a 15-minute planning meeting (with yourself) in the diary, towards the end of every day, during working time. Usually this is best in the afternoon or early evening, so that you go to sleep knowing the next day will be valuable and well-paced, as well as allowing time for the unexpected
- During this planning meeting, begin by reviewing your long list and then developing your 4-6 priorities for the next day (definitely no more than 6)

I use technology all the time to increase my time planning effectiveness. Here's how:

- I keep a long list in an Outlook note so it is next to my calendar.
- At the top of the long list, I write a summary of the time mastery method that is in this post
- (Here's the key point) I do not put my daily plan in this Outlook note; instead, the calendar functions as my daily to-do list
- I use nudges and the 'do' button on my Apple Watch and notifications on my phone, to remind me of key transitions, e.g. the start of a period of time for sport

The most important thing is focus. During the working day, as things come up that are important but not urgent (or urgent but not important) remind yourself why your planned priorities are paramount. Also think about the satisfaction you will gain by completing all of your tasks.

Why do these steps work? Researchers at Oxford University found that groups who multi-tasked performed the tasks more slowly and less accurately. Simply put, the three steps are about focusing on one thing at a time. Do that and your productivity will skyrocket! Now it's over to you.

Managing your energy
– the energy map

Tor Mesoy, Hong Kong

One of the characteristics of effective leaders is that they are good at managing their energy. This is a complex topic, and it requires practice. It starts with self-awareness: What is my energy level now – physically, mentally, emotionally, spiritually? And why? Do I want to change it? When? And how?

In addition to self-awareness, we need to know how to build and restore energy. It includes exercise, nutrition, intellectual stimulation, breaks at regular intervals, relating deeply to friends, and connecting with the profound sense of meaning in our lives.

We cannot be at peak performance all the time, so important leadership disciplines include managing our communication with others and our impact on others when we are feeling low, and managing our cycle so that we can deliver when it really counts. One way to visualize this is with the energy map developed by Loehr and Schwartz — the simple two-by-two depicted below.

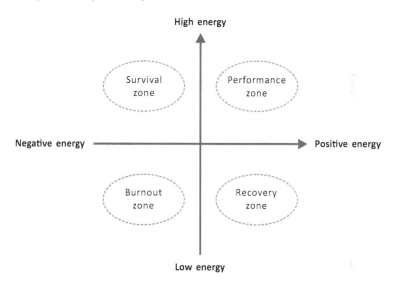

It is incredibly helpful to know which quadrant we are in at any time, and to know when and how to move from one quadrant to the next. We do not have absolute control of where in the map we find ourselves, but through conscious interventions, we can influence our position and move from one quadrant to a more desirable one.

This spring has been very busy for me. I have been in the Performance zone much of the time. I have zipped around the Americas, Europe and Asia, delivering leadership seminars, facilitating top team alignment workshops, hosting webinars, giving talks, designing culture change interventions, coaching executives, attending board meetings and much more. It has been exhilarating. I managed to stay in the Performance zone for about six months. Sure, I was sometimes tired and jet-lagged, but I would bounce back quickly when I found myself in front of a new group of people where I had the opportunity to inspire, stretch, challenge, and encourage.

And then it hit me. I slid into the Survival zone where I was dragging my body to work every day; driven more by habit and a sense of professional obligation than by true inspiration. I believe it was the combination of two disappointing events that triggered this change. It is often like that, isn't it? We can tackle a single challenge, but when they pile up, we struggle, especially if we have been running hard for a while. In my case it was the combination of a professional disappointment — an interesting project postponed by my client — and a personal set-back — unexpected strife with a long-time friend.

After dragging my body to work for a while, I knew that I had slipped further – into the *Burnout zone*. I knew that I needed to take conscious steps to recover. Here is what I did: I shared with my wife how I was feeling, and asked her for space, for patience and for support. Simply naming where we are at often helps. I got back into a better rhythm of exercising, and would go running several times a week. I caught up on sleep. I made sure to eat better – fruit and vegetables at regular hours rather than fast food gulped down at airports at odd hours. I stepped back and reframed my view of the situation. I chose to view this time of lower professional intensity (because the client project had been postponed) as a gift, a true blessing. I took time to catch up on professional literature and finished several books that had been on my list for a long time. I reconnected with friends in a very intentional manner. Specifically, I reached out to several of them and expressed my gratitude for what they represented in my life. And at the time of writing this, I sense I am moving back into the Performance zone again. One indicator: today's morning run felt light – the photo accompanying this article is a shot of sunrise over Victoria Harbor, Hong Kong, taken this morning at 6AM.

As I watched the sun break through the clouds, I was filled with an immense sense of gratitude. I was grateful to have the chance to experience the beauty of the harbor this quiet morning. I was grateful that the run was going smoothly. I was grateful for the sense of surplus energy and the drive to take on new challenges.

A friend of mine recently said: "I love growing old!" Her exclamation touched me. As she aged, she felt more centered, more conscious, wiser. Her statement resonates with me. As we grow older, we may hope to get smarter about managing our energy. I know for a fact that when I was younger, I squandered my energy in all kinds of silly ways – driven by a wish for external recognition or driven by anxiety. Not productive at all.

I started this post by stating that managing energy is a complex topic. There are many facets to this topic, and it is good investment to explore these facets so that we can steward our energy effectively. And, fortunately, there are a lot of resources to tap into. A friend of mine, Tim Zak, does a podcast on how to unlock the secrets of high performance: www.insearchoflostmojo.com. Check it out! The first episode (https://timzak.com/islm-1-eugster/) is with Dr. Charles Eugster, a British world-record holding athlete, body builder, and author of *Age Is Just a Number: What a 97 Year Old Record Breaker Can Teach Us About Growing Older*.

Whatever our age, mastering the art and science of managing our energy enables us to more consistently be at our best. It's worth our time to deepen our understanding and hone our skills in this critical area.

Are you in the flow?

Tor Mesoy, Hong Kong

"Let yourself be silently drawn by the strange pull of what you really love. It will not lead you astray." — Rumi

I am richly blessed: I love my work. I get a thrill out of supporting leaders to become the best they can be. Going on a journey of discovery with a client to explore potential, hidden talents, blind spots, and options is deeply rewarding to me. Nurturing and encouraging clients to tackle challenges in new ways is intensely meaningful. Hearing their reflections as they grow in understanding and insight is often hugely inspiring. Receiving news on the breakthroughs they have achieved is enormously energizing.

In deep coaching conversations with clients, I often experience a state of "flow" – the special feeling in a high-challenge situation where you use yourself to the utmost of your abilities and apply all your skills and experience … in such a way that it seems effortless.

Mihaly Csikszentmihalyi studied flow over a long period and highlights seven characteristics of being in flow:

  1: Complete involvement in what we are doing – focus, concentration
  2: A sense of ecstasy – of being outside daily reality
  3: Great inner clarity – knowing what needs to be done, and how well we are doing
  4: The knowledge that the activity is doable – that our skills are adequate to the task
  5: A sense of serenity – no worries about oneself, and a feeling of growing beyond the boundaries of ego
  6: Timelessness – thoroughly focused on the present, hours seem to pass by in minutes
  7: Intrinsic motivation – whatever produces flow becomes its own rewards

As I work with my clients, I wish, intensely, that they might regularly experience flow. Sadly, this is not common. People often feel stuck in a dead-end job that does not challenge them. Or, they experience very challenging situations but do not have the mastery required to tackle these situations, and become victims of circumstance. Regularly, people feel stuck in well-compensated jobs that they do not find inspiring, but they struggle to articulate the vision to break free. They struggle to find the courage to step out.

Friends: life here on earth is short. Do not settle for mediocrity. You were gifted with talents, skills and passion for a purpose. Keep looking until you find the sweet spot where three circles overlap: your strengths, your passion and the needs of your organization, so that you regularly experience flow.

If you know what your strengths and your passion are, but there is poor fit with your current organization, find another organization where you can invest yourself and find fulfilment.

If there is a good match between your passion and the organization you are in, but your struggle to deliver what is expected of you, build the additional skills required for true mastery, so that you can excel and experience flow.

If you are doing well in your current organization, using your skills optimally, but your heart is not in it, beware. You may come to regret your loyalty. Investigate what you are being loyal to, and explore how you can live out your passion more fully.

Where and when do YOU experience flow? What can you do to savor this experience more frequently?

The exciting inner journey of discovery

Tor Mesoy, Hong Kong

"The longest journey is the journey inward." — Dag Hammarskjöld

I am a keen kayaker. I have had the joy of paddling kayaks around the world – in the US, in South Africa, in New Zealand, in Norway and in Greenland. My most spectacular kayaking trip was perhaps a trip among the icebergs along the west coast of Greenland, starting in Ilulissat. The icebergs were sometimes beautiful – in shades from white through baby blue to deep teal. And sometimes they were enormous. The largest one we passed was a roughly hewn cube with sides of two kilometers. We would regularly observe a huge chunk of ice break off from the top of an iceberg, and then see the iceberg, now destabilized, turn majestically around in the water to find a new equilibrium – sending waves out in all directions.

At one point, we paddled quite close to an iceberg when we heard a loud, cracking sound. We expected this sound to be accompanied by something more, but nothing happened. Nothing happened — for a while, that is. After about ten seconds, a mini-iceberg came rushing up from the deep, broke the surface, and lazily turned over on its side. The new iceberg had broken off from the main one, deep under the surface and, being lighter than water, had floated to the surface, where it sent a gush of foam and water in all directions. We figured it was time to get out of there, lest further instability would have more dire consequences for fragile kayakers.

I am grateful for the opportunity to learn about icebergs along the coast of Greenland. Even more exciting, though, has been what I have learned about the iceberg that each one of us represents. We observe the behaviors of people around us, including their speech and their gestures. These behaviors give us some inkling about what goes on beneath the surface, but there is often much more than we perceive. The metaphor of the iceberg is therefore apt. The iceberg reveals around a tenth of itself above the water surface. The rest is hidden beneath the surface. In a similar way, people only show a small part of themselves; most of who they are remains hidden. Through respectful and gentle probing, we can uncover some of it – thereby deepening our understanding and vastly improving commu-nication and collaboration.

What are the components of people hidden beneath the surface? Assumptions (some warranted, some perhaps not), anxieties, fears, needs (some met, some perhaps not) and much more.

My wife and I were raised in different cultures. She was raised in a low-trust culture; I was raised in a high-trust culture. She was taught to nurture harmony; I was taught to "speak truth to power". She was raised with collectivist values; I was raised with a strong emphasis on the value of the individual. Hence, I am regularly baffled by her behavior (and I know I regularly baffle her). But knowing that we have such different backgrounds sometimes makes it easier for us to acknowledge our differences and to remain curious – rather than getting frustrated or angry. Paradoxically, it can actually be easier to communicate with someone from a different culture, as we avoid the illusion that we (fully) know and understand the other. When working with someone from our own environment and culture, it is easier to fall in the trap of writing off a surprising behavior as stupid or immature without taking the time to explore what drives the behavior. When communicating with my wife, I consciously force myself to retain an open mind and to ask "Why?" when her behavior, her words, her priorities surprise me. Sometimes I use gentler words, since "why" can be a bit harsh and can easily be interpreted as the start of an inquisition or an accusation. "What leads to you to say this?" can work better. Or, perhaps, "Help me understand what makes you prioritize this way". And as I practice with my wife, I am getting better at staying curious with other people too – including the ones who are culturally closer to me.

How does this work in practice in the professional world? Let me offer an example. At one time I served a hospital chain that was working to renew its IT infrastructure. This was a critical endeavor, as much of the hardware equipment was so old that it was no longer supported by the vendor. Many software solutions had passed the official end-of-life date of the provider. The amount of systems downtime was increasing, thereby jeopardizing the lives of patients. Regularly, patients could not be admitted because the admissions system was down. Or surgery could not be performed because the scheduling system that matched patient, surgeon and surgery was unavailable. The situation was dire. In addition to the risk to the life and safety of patients, there was another cost: by skimping on capital expenditure, the hospital had dramatically increased its IT operating expense; it was becoming inordinately expensive to operate their aging IT infrastructure.

While budgets were tight, there was little doubt that some renewal was required. The hospital put together the estimates and the business case for this. I got the job to meet with physicians and build support for this investment. The meeting was memorable. I had scheduled the meeting with two representatives for the medical doctors, but when I came to the meeting room, there were 20 people present. They listened in cold silence as I laid out the case for renewal. Then they voiced their perspective that this was entirely unnecessary. I was struck. I had just laid out the case that the hospital was incurring very high costs, unnecessarily, and that patients' lives were in danger. And here were these doctors saying that there was no need for change. It would have been easy to dismiss their position as "stupid" (perhaps using a different term). Instead, I probed to understand what was going on. It took more than the one meeting, but by asking "why?", level by level I got to understand the doctors' stance. It was actually logical. At least, there was an internal logic to

their position. It was this: Any investment in IT may yield real benefits, but these are uncertain (the money might be wasted along the
way) and they are likely to only materialize several years in the future.
On the other hand, money made available now can be used to buy
expensive oncology medicines that will prolong the lives of patients
who are in the hospital today. These individuals have names, faces
and families – they are real. Weighing up future uncertain benefits
against the very real benefits that were available now, the physicians'
choice was clear.

It would have been easy to dismiss the physicians' initial position. But
curiosity about what was beneath the surface together with some
patience plus some gentle probing made it possible to create the
arena for an intelligent conversation. People are always more open to
considering your perspective when they sense that they have been
heard and understood.

I am writing this on the plane on my way to my next destination,
having just facilitated a leadership development program for a group
of 20 senior leaders from a dozen different countries. The program
was energizing and inspiring because the participants chose to remain
curious – while also being supportive of one another. They were good
at probing, gently and respectfully, to understand the aspirations, the
hopes and the fears that their fellow participants harbored. This
made them effective at challenging and supporting one another. And
this, in turn, helped the participants gain a deeper understanding of
themselves, of their objectives and of the next steps on their journey.
This clarity will make them more inspiring as leaders in years to come.
They will be more inspiring because they will be more inspired. And

they will be more inspired because they have more courage. And the courage will come from increased clarity. And the clarity comes from curiosity and persistence.

As leaders, we can make a huge difference by remaining aware that there is critical insight lurking "beneath the surface." This applies to other people – whom we do not fully understand – and it applies to ourselves. For we do not fully understand ourselves: our implicit assumptions, our scars, our hopes, our fears, our needs. If we approach situations of conflict and tension with curiosity, with generosity and with kindness, we can gain rich insight, uncover untold riches, unleash great potential and create tremendous value. Let us help one another in this quest.

Finding the courage to say "no"
– gently and respectfully

Tor Mesoy, Austria

"A 'NO' spoken from the deepest conviction is better than a 'yes' uttered merely to please..." – Mahatma Gandhi

This week I have been running a leadership development program in Central Europe. I feel privileged to be able to spend a week in a pleasant environment and help participants explore more of who they are, who they want to become, how they can become more effective in their leadership roles and how they can clear hurdles that stand in their way. We do this in group settings and one-on-one coaching.

Several of the participants shared that one thing that stands in their way is that they regularly experience conflicting commitments. They feel torn by requests and expectations coming from many different directions, and they struggle to say "no". They end up living up to the vision that someone else has for their lives rather than fulfilling their own dreams.

Participants shared a number of tactical hints on how to say "no" smartly: "Explain to the requester that you are already committed to something else", "Express that you would really like to help but you are already stretched", "Negotiate a later dateline for delivering on the request", and "State that you want to provide support, but that you will need resources to do so." The list continues. Many of these suggestions are good, but they do not address the root cause of the conflict that many feel.

One of the participants nailed it when she expressed what lay behind the concern: Fear. Fear of what they will think of me — "Is she not hard-working?" Fear of what they will say — "Is he not prepared to take one for the team?". Fear of poor evaluations. Fear of postponed promotion. Fear of being fired. And living in fear is detrimental to any exercise of leadership. It is hard to be inspirational when you are scared.

Now, courage is not the absence of fear, but the realization that something else is more important, more valuable. How can we gather the courage to say "no" – gently, respectfully – rather than compromise on our principles and sacrifice our plans, our priorities? The key seems to be a combination of self-awareness and a strong sense of purpose. We need the self-awareness to recognize the lurking fear, name it and understand where it comes from. This is the starting point for testing assumptions and reframing how we view the request and the requester. But this is not sufficient. We also need a strong, personal sense of purpose. This is what we say "yes" to when we say "no" to something else. If this sense of purpose is fuzzy, it is very hard to say "no". When this sense of purpose is clear and well-articulated, it gives us the strength and the courage to give ourselves permission to say "no" to requests which are unreasonable, arbitrary or simply not aligned with what we are aiming for.

This is of course not an invitation to be self-centered and navel-gazing and only look out for ourselves. But it is the basis for living centered lives where we pursue our personal vision rather being buffeted helplessly by forces around us. The world will be a better place when our primary motivation is compelling vision rather than fear. Take time to deepen self-awareness and strengthen personal sense of purpose, and encourage those you love to do the same.

Three ways to make the most of your success

Nick Chatrath, Oxford

I am writing this article with a smile on my face, because I just received the news that I have been accredited by the Association for Coaching at the highest level, Master Executive Coach. This required 1,500 hours of logged coaching practice, recording my coaching for evaluation, and a 1.5-year process of preparing my portfolio (which ran to 100 pages).

This marks the end of an even longer journey for me. In 2003 when I started my own coaching practice, I considered pursuing an accreditation, but never followed through. Clients weren't demanding it, and I hadn't yet realized the centrality of supervision and a reflective approach to great coaching. It took Oxford University's Saïd Business

School, where I am a member of the coaching community, to prompt me to apply for accreditation. I'm so glad they did, because – as I tell my supervisor Jean Dowson – the process of reflection and supervision has improved my coaching practice significantly. I'm sure you are happy for me, but why am I telling you this?

I realized that we can all learn from three aspects of my reaction to receiving the news about my accreditation.

1: Celebrate

So many of us don't take time to celebrate. In so much of our lives we are climbing ladders. When we climb one rung, how often do we stop and celebrate our success? When I received the news about my accreditation, I initially told some friends. Their sheer delight made me stop and think, "Hang on, why don't I take time to celebrate this?" So I did.

What about you?

Look back over the last 12 months of your life. What is there to celebrate? Pause, reflect and be thankful for this.

2: Use success to understand more deeply what drives you

Why does a child get excited when they get their 5-metre swimming badge? Often it's not that they've shown themselves that they can do it, but that they have shown others they can do it. I noticed that some of my delight at being accredited came from my desire to be seen or known. My delight also stemmed from how important coaching had been in my life, even from my earliest years. I recall now that, at the age of 10, a teacher asked me to coach a fellow pupil on spelling. And years before I started calling myself a coach, I gravitated to helping others through questions, in my first job.

The happiest people and the most successful people connect what they do with who they are. They have reflected on where they fit best. They are clear on what skills they have, and how this links to their purpose.

What about you?
Maybe you like connecting people, or managing projects, or adminis-tering things. Trace your journey back and consider 2-3 of your major successes. What have you always known about yourself? Identify one thing that you can change about your current life or work, that will bring what you do more into line with who you are.

3: Use success as a platform to keep learning, not as a finishing line to protect
After receiving a badge of success, it is tempting to stop trying and to think "I've made it. I can kick back now, and don't need to learn." This is fatal to both success and happiness, as lack of learning turns quickly into boredom and underperformance. For me, using success as a platform for learning means contributing to the coaching profession by developing new coaching models that will allow more people access to high quality coaching.

What about you?
Where in your life have you stopped learning? Where in your life do you need to learn most? Consider what you need to do next as a result.

Whenever you receive good news, make the most of it.

Chapter 3
Leading others

" A leader is best when people barely know he exists... when his work is done, his aim fulfilled, they will all say: we did it ourselves."

— Lao Tzu

The value of letting go of control

Tor Mesoy, Denmark

Henry Kissinger, still going strong at 93, expressed "Power is the ultimate aphrodisiac." [Quote from *The New York Times*, 28 Oct 1973]. Whatever our desired end is, we regularly get enamored with power and control. But power and control regularly give us a false sense of security and get in the way of our ultimate objectives. This insight should give us pause, so we step back and develop a better perspective on our desire for power and control.

Recently, I ran a leadership development program just outside Copenhagen. With a group of leaders, I explored how to build and strengthen strategic, trust-based relationships. One of the ways we explored was to be genuinely curious, listen deeply and ask open-ended questions, for example:

- What are you aspiring to?
- What (about this) makes you most excited?
- What concerns you most?
- What would the ideal outcome (of this initiative) look like?
- What would happen if you did nothing?

It is of course not about rattling off these questions. It is about being genuinely curious, listening in an appreciative manner and giving the other person space to think and to speak, freely. When we do this well, we open up the space for the other person and we may help them understand more about themselves and about how they relate to the world.

One of the participants in the leadership development program (let us call him Walter) looked at this list of questions and balked: "But if I ask these kinds of questions, the other person may go off on a tangent, and I might lose control of the meeting."

A poignant moment. After a pregnant pause, the conversation went (roughly) like this:

I: "Walter, when you speak with you wife, do you seek to always be in control?"
Walter: "No, of course not."
I: "Why?"
Walter: "Well, she would not like that and it would signal a low level of trust."
I: "Hmm. Yes, I see that... How do you think it works in a profes-

sional setting, when you seek to maintain tight *control* of a dialog?"

Walter saw the connection and gained a new perspective on his desire to "be in control". In a good conversation, all participants are learning something new, but this requires full presence and it involves listening with an open mind and an open heart.

Otto Scharmer, senior lecturer at MIT, describes four levels of listening:

Level 1: Downloading: At this level we are mainly attuned to reconfirming our biases. We do not expect to learn anything new. Sometimes we follow social protocol and we refrain from interrupting, but in reality, we are merely waiting to present our rebuttal.

Level 2: Factual listening: At this level, we pay attention to facts and data. We are prepared to learn, but the learning is quite superficial.

Level 3: Empathetic listening: At this deeper level, we engage in real dialog and we pay careful attention to body language, tone of voice, pitch and pace to discern where the other person is coming from. This represents a profound shift in the place from which our listening originates. This allows us to see how the world appears through the other person's eyes.

Level 4: Generative listening: At this most profound level, we slow down and all participants listen to what is said and to what is not said, to the possibilities that might emerge from that which is shared. Scharmer uses the term "grace" to describe the texture of this experience. That might sound esoteric, but we know it when we experience it. And we know that such listening can trigger truly transformative new insights. And we know that such listening is antithetical to "being in control". No one is "in control" when we listen to one another at this deep level.

Another way to come at this is the following take on three ways to ask questions. Think about the question "Why did you do this?" and imagine someone asking it in the following three ways:

1: We can ask as an *investigator*, perhaps seeking to apportion blame or responsibility
2: We can ask as a *scientist*, dispassionately seeking to uncover the facts, to understand linkages
3: ... or we can ask as a *lover*, at a romantic dinner, in a quest to connect deeply to the other person, to fully appreciate and savor the value of the other, to understand in order to build unity and a common future

Asking as an investigator or as a scientist is entirely compatible with "being in control". Asking as a lover is not. While the metaphor is simple, we – and the people we work with – might benefit from shifting our listening to the deeper level.

The conversation with Walter made me reflect deeply: where can I, personally, let go of control to a greater extent, and explore with an open mind, an open heart and an open will? I sense that there is much more to discover, and I want to practice, systematically.

Managing conflict
– slowing down to speed up

Tor Mesoy, Beijing

Last weekend I was in Beijing on a mission. I was invited to contribute to resolving a personal conflict between two parties, a conflict that had been going on for years. The setting was interesting – and challenging – for several reasons, but one stands out: the two parties and I did not share a common language. This meant that everything had to be translated – substantially slowing down proceedings. We did not have a professional interpreter who could provide real-time interpreting. Rather, each sentence was translated after it was spoken.

There was a distinct possibility that this would be awkward. Resolving conflict depends on mutual understanding, and it would be easy to think that the lack of a common language would seriously impede progress. As it turns out, we made great progress; the parties achieved a real breakthrough.

Reflecting on this, it struck me that we turned what looked like an impediment – the lack of a common language – into a strength. Because everything had to be translated, it gave people time to reflect. It gave the speaker, at any moment, time to think carefully about how to phrase the next part of their explanation, while the previous argument was being translated. It gave the listener time to digest the most recently translated argument, while the next statement was spoken. This forced time for reflection had a huge impact.

Naturally, this was not the sole key to the breakthrough. Other important factors include a conducive environment (a private room in a wonderful Japanese-style teahouse), mutual respect, willingness to listen, skillful acknowledgement of what was heard, expression of empathy and creativity. Nevertheless, the forced slowing-down imposed by the language gap was a key success factor.

How can we use this learning in other settings – the more common conflict settings where everyone does share a common language? I suggest four approaches.

The first approach is straightforward. You can unilaterally decide to reduce your own pace. You can use shorter sentences, slow your speech and take longer pauses. This will give everyone in the room more time to reflect. This will very likely affect the other parties, and you will see them mirror your behavior – slowing down. This will happen, quite naturally, even without any explicit conversation about pace.

The second approach is more explicit. At the start of the conversation, take time to acknowledge that this will be a difficult conversation and re-confirm that all involved parties are keen to understand one another and to find a solution. Then agree some ground rules for the conversation. This might include something about reducing the pace, taking time to reflect along the way and consciously acknowledging the contributions from other parties. This approach may work better if there is a third party in the room – a mediator, a counselor or some other trusted party that can facilitate the discussion. It will often be easier for such a facilitator to create the arena for a productive dialog, and to help ensure that everyone slows down. But, with practice, this can also be done without a facilitator, provided the parties trust one another.

The third approach is more formal. It involves using a talking stick, also called a speaker's staff. The stick confers the right to speak to the person holding the stick. This is a practice used in council meetings of traditional communities, especially those of indigenous peoples of the Northwest Coast of North America. The talking stick can be a beautiful, ornate, custom-made stick. It can also be any item of suitable size that can be held in the hand and passed around. Using a talking stick feels artificial in the beginning, but people typically get used to it within fifteen minutes, provided they have an open mind and are inclined to try something different. Using the talking stick slows things down – there is necessarily a pause when the stick is passed from one person to another. It also makes it clearer when someone is hogging the air space or someone is not participating. Offering the stick to a quiet person can be a way to get them involved.

The fourth and most radical approach can be seen as a simulation of the setting where everything is translated into another language. It involves using a talking stick, and takes the concept one step further. Now, after I have spoken for a short while, I pause, and I invite you to echo back to me what you heard, in your own words. Only when I feel heard, do I continue. When I have completed what I had to say – and you have echoed back to me what you heard at regular intervals – I pass the stick to you. Now it is your turn to speak and my turn to reflect back to you what I am hearing, seeking confirmation that I am hearing you correctly. This takes some getting used to. But it is a powerful technique to break out of established, dysfunctional patterns where people are speaking, but not listening.

In the coming week, pick an important and difficult conversation you are having, and slow down – using one of the approaches I have sketched. You may find that you reach results faster. Slowing down is a powerful way to speed up conflict resolution.

Being effective in difficult, high-stakes conversations: three hints

Tor Mesoy, Hong Kong

Some of the leaders I coach struggle with a common challenge: they come across as tense and awkward when facing senior leadership or in those tough negotiation meetings where the outcome is critical. The more important the outcome of the conversation, the more gauche they seem – regularly to the point where they self-destruct and doom the conversation to failure from the start. Sometimes the awkward behavior is blatant. Sometimes it is quite subtle, but it is sufficient for the parties to get into a negative spiral. What is going on? You might think that when the stakes are high, these leaders should be able to pull themselves together and come across as centered, calm and peer-like, but this is often not easy.

One leader I recently observed seemed eager to please, to the point of being subservient. With words and with body language he seemed to be asking: "Do you approve of what I am telling you now? "Do you approve of me?" "Do you like what you are hearing now?"

Another ended up reading from copious notes, thereby killing any semblance of authenticity and of owning the story and the argument. The implicit message was: "I don't really know my stuff very well. I am a messenger who relies on my notes to get the information across."

A third leader seemed apologetic about not having full control of all the facts – in an early, exploratory dialog where no one actually had any such expectations. Whenever a question came up, he would refrain from engaging in a dialog about the topic, but would close down the conversation by saying something like "I don't know that. I will have to get back to you."

In each of these cases, these leaders signaled strongly to their counterparts that they were not worthy of serious consideration. The signaling stems from their own perception that they are, somehow, not worthy. And this rapidly and predictably becomes self-fulfilling. Their counterparts react to the cues intuitively and often subconsciously, and treat these leaders with less respect. The leaders end up achieving limited impact or they end up with a poor negotiation result.

A colleague of mine, who is more deeply into neuroscience than I am, surmises that what is happening is that these leaders trigger the firing of mirror neurons in the minds of their counterparts. Through this mechanism, they create uncertainty in the minds of the counterparts, and this is rarely a good starting point for subtle communication, trust-building and creative, win-win negotiations. I am not fully convinced of this model. It is an intriguing hypothesis, but I have not seen authoritative research that validates this account. But perhaps this does not matter so much. Reality, as I have observed it, is compatible with this explanatory model, and the model may give us some ideas for how to deal with the challenge I have sketched.

How should you prepare for a difficult conversation where you perceive that you are the weaker party or the junior party? In my work with executives and other leaders have observed three techniques that work well:
    1: Challenge the perception
    2: Take the ego out of it
    3: Be in the moment

1: Challenge the perception
The perception that you are the weaker party sometimes stems from a difference in age or a difference in length-of-experience or a difference position in a formal hierarchy. But these factors are generally less critical than they might seem. A younger person who introduces a bright idea should not feel inferior because of age. It is the quality of the idea that matters. An executive who challenges a recommendation from the CEO should combat any sense of insecurity because of the formal hierarchy that exists, it is the depth of insight that counts.

2: Take the ego out of it

We are typically far too focused on what people think of us. People's perceptions do, of course, matter. If we did not care at all, we might cause offense, or we might hurt people. So, a healthy interest in how others react to our words and our actions is a good thing. But too often, our ego gets wrapped up in this. Our focus ends up being on how others will judge us, whether we will rise or fall in their esteem. This ego-centric perspective can be damaging. I have found that simply acknowledging this can help us control the inner voices that speak about such esteem. Before we enter a high-stakes or difficult conversation, we might gain from reflecting on what is truly at stake here. More often than not, this will help us find the courage to have the conversation in a more relaxed manner – taking the ego out of it. A friend of mine has a little ritual. As he crosses the threshold on his way into a difficult, high-stakes meeting, he will whisper, under his breath: "It's not about me".

3: Be in the moment

In difficult conversations, our minds can sometimes be all over the place. Our inner voices may be talking about the disastrous consequences if this dialog does not go well. They may be talking about how inadequate our preparation is. This is not helpful. It detracts from our capacity to listen deeply to the other person. It helps if we can silence these voices for a while. Different mindfulness practices can support us in this regard. For some, this may mean prayer. For others, it may mean meditation. For others, again, it may be a visualization exercise where you envisage what a great conversation this can be. The key point is to help ensure that we are more fully present, here and now. Ready to listen, ready to engage, ready to share based on what is transpiring in the dialog. It takes practice, but the payback is high.

Next time you are facing a difficult dialog, prepare productively. Challenge the assumptions that lead you to believe that this is difficult. Take your ego out of it. Be in the moment. Perhaps you will trigger positive firing patterns in the mirror neurons of the other person and you will jointly generate new, creative insights that will generate huge value and lay a great foundation for future collaboration. Best wishes!

Discovering the deep value of checking in

Tor Mesoy, Hong Kong

Many years ago, I started to work with a sociologist. It was an eye-opening experience. Until that time, I had mainly worked with people who had their education in mathematics, computer science, natural sciences and business. I had collaborated with the odd lawyer and the odd medical doctor, but a sociologist was something new. And different.

My new colleague (and, later, friend) would, every time we met, share with me how he was feeling and what was going on in his life. Sometimes he would share happy moments and little victories. Sometimes he would share troubles, challenges and difficulties. At first, this was odd to me. It seemed almost child-like. I would nod politely while he shared his status, with a wan smile, often feeling mildly uncomfortable. It was as if I was invited and led into a living room where I did not really belong.

But his behavior grew on me. Gradually, I started to look forward to his sharing, candidly and vulnerably, what was important to him. As our relationship deepened and our trust grew, I felt that I could ask him about his habit. At one level, it seemed entirely natural to him, but I was convinced that it was a conscious choice to live his life so openly. He confirmed this. To him, this was a way to connect more deeply as human beings. While he did not expect others to adopt his style, he clearly sensed that he was role-modeling something important and that his sharing represented an invitation to others to be, more fully, themselves. I started to experiment with this. When we met, I would share, more openly, what was going on in my own life. This accelerated our trust building and it rapidly made for a richer relationship.

I recently led a leadership program in Hanoi. One of the participating leaders, Kate, shared that while she had had a successful career, she had recently moved to a new position where expectations were different, and she was receiving poor upward feedback. She had paid extra attention to following up her people, but this had not helped much. I asked how she followed up her people, and she shared that she would check on their progress, ask if they needed help with their tasks and check if they were on track to deliver on their targets. She would do this in a supportive way, truly wanting all her people to succeed. I had an inkling what the issue might be. It seemed that she was only providing support at the intellectual level. And she was only checking in at the intellectual level. We explored this together, and she left our program excited to open up a new space.

We humans are whole, integrated beings, with mind, body and soul. We have intellectual, emotional and spiritual needs. All too often our work places, however, pay scant attention to anything but our intellectual contribution and our intellectual needs. We provide training to our people, and give them information, frameworks, models and tools – all addressing the intellectual side. And our work places remain emotionally and spiritually, barren wastelands.

When we check in with people – be they peers, followers or leaders – it is valuable to see them as they are – whole, integrated beings, with mind, body and soul. This is the perspective that is embedded in the Zulu greeting "Sawubona," which is often translated as "hello", but rendered, literally as "I see you". What a wonderful greeting! "I see you ... in all your humanity: your strengths, your weaknesses, your hurts, your aspirations, your hopes, your yearnings, your victories, your joy." Without prying, it is enriching to be open to all these facets – not just where people stand "in terms of meeting their targets." And we can signal our openness to others by sharing more of what is going in our lives – like my sociologist friend did.

There are many ways to check in, even if we restrict our exchanges to the professional domain. It is legitimate to ask: "Is your work giving you joy? What would you need to get more fulfillment from it?" It is straightforward to inquire: "To what extent are you meeting some of your personal aspirations as you engage in this work?" or "Are you continuing to learn and grow in your current role? What would it take for you to learn and grow the way you want to?"

A friend of mine, Brechje van Geenen, recently shared the way she checks in with people. When she gets together with another person, she encourages them both to answer three simple questions:

1: How am I feeling right now?
2: What is keeping me from being fully present?
3: What is my intention for this meeting?

I find that beautiful. It opens up a huge space – respectfully. It builds connection. It fosters belonging. It avoids misunderstandings. What a tremendous investment of time and energy – to ask these three simple questions ... and then to listen deeply. Not problem solving with the other, not showing sympathy, not criticizing – merely accepting and acknowledging. And seeing the other.

Another friend of mine, Irina, shared a different notion of checking in. She was focusing on the challenge of a loving, married couple to stay close – decade after decade, as they grew and changed, individually. Her starting point was provocative: "You are married to a different person each year. The person you were married to last year, no longer exists. They have matured, they have experienced new things and they are, now, literally a different person." Unless you do something special, you risk drifting apart, and one day you ask the question that "Schmidt" (Jack Nicholson) asks in the movie About Schmidt: "Who is this old woman who lives in my house?" A possible antidote, Irina suggested, was to ask a single question of one another, every day: "What is the most important thing that happened to you today, and how did it make you feel?" At the end of a year, you have 365 data points that give you an excellent basis for understanding who the other person is.

Whether it is at work or at play, let us check in with one another in a meaningful manner. Find your way to check in, and make the world a better place, locally, around you, by simply seeing the people around you in their full humanity.

For a fresh perspective,
get on the balcony

Lucy Qian, Shenzhen

"Activity is obstructive to liberation, as any results obtained are impermanent, thus creating more bondage." – Shri Ramananda Mayi

Recently I coached Annie (to protect confidentiality, I have changed the name) on an issue that she had been wrestling with for years. When she began to talk, she rapidly burst into tears. But after a short while I was thrilled when she walked out of the session with a great sense of release, feeling positive and appreciative.

As I reflected on our coaching conversation, one particular moment stood out for me. As Annie described her situation, I noticed she was torn between her competing needs. On the one hand, she wished she could see changes happen in her extended family members so that they could manage conflicts with one another in a more peaceful manner. On the other hand, she loved her family so much that she wanted to accept them as they were. She was anxious, as she thought that these needs could not co-exist and she had to choose which one to address. I asked her to swap seats with me. When she sat in my seat, I asked her to talk to the part of her that was desperate for a change in her family members. After that, I asked her to swap back and talk to the other part of her, the one that wanted to hold her family in unconditionally positive regard. As she spoke, she slowed down and looked as if she was talking to another person. As I was about to ask a question, she stood up, walked over to the wall, leant against it, and started talking to "both parts of herself". This time she was calmer. It seemed as if the physical distance she had secured by leaving her seat had given her a completely new perspective. She seemed less engrossed in her own problems, but was able to contemplate them as if from the outside. As she finished, I noticed an emerging smile on her face; she looked content and peaceful. She later shared that it was from that moment she felt she was in control of her situation.

This experience reminded me of a leadership concept introduced by Ronald Heifetz - "balcony and dance floor". As a leader, your effectiveness depends on your ability to observe and synthesize a complex set of signs and data that are often conflicting. You must be attuned to what is critical, what is at stake, what your team really needs, and what is emerging. A useful strategy to stay on top of those undercurrents is to periodically step back from your need to do something and assess your attachment to results. Picture yourself leaving the "dance floor" where you are busy with action, and "getting on the balcony", so that you can observe the action, your team and yourself. Just as in the coaching example: getting on the balcony helped Annie gain perspective in the midst of her competing needs. Achieving some distance from her struggle and engaging with the two different parts of her allowed new insights and solutions to emerge. Your ability as a leader to gain perspective on a challenging situation allows you to connect with the root cause with greater ease.

However, as a leader, not only do you need to get on the balcony yourself, you also need to help your team do it from time to time. You may say that this might be easier if you were a professional coach. It actually does not require you to be an expert in coaching. Success hinges on preparation, and you can prepare in four simple ways.

1: Set your intention and focus

Your intention determines where your focus is. When team members come to you with a problem, as a leader, if your intention is to solve the problem for them, you will naturally focus on the drama and the details within the problem. However, if you intend to develop their ability to solve problems, you will focus on the person: on his or her motivation and needs, mindsets and perspectives, strengths and resources. When you focus on the problem, you encourage your team remain on the dance floor. When you help them focus on their vision and strategies, and guide them to identify their own solutions, you direct your team to get on the balcony.

2: Ask honest, open questions

Honest, open questions expand rather than restrict self-exploration. They do not push or even nudge people toward a particular way of framing a situation. They should come from a desire to support the other's self-exploration, rather than from a need to fix a situation or a person. Through asking honest, open questions, you help your team to get some distance from the challenging situation in order to gain perspective, just as in the coaching example in the beginning. Such questions are not difficult to ask, when you set your intention well. Here are some examples: "What will success look like for you in this project?", "How will you know when you have achieved your goal?", "How can you build on what is already working?".

3: Listen deeply

In his book *Theory U: leading from the future as it emerges*, Otto Scharmer introduces four levels of listening. He describes the deepest level as "generative listening" where you are connected to "something larger than yourself" and sense the "highest future possibility that can emerge". When you access this level of listening, you are working at the systems level. You treat every statement someone makes as a signal from the whole system that is trying to grab your attention. With this mindset, you are able to get some distance from the issues or complaints your team brings to you. You resist the temptation to know every detail of the issues. As you filter the noise, you increase the chance of hearing what your team really thinks, what their perspectives are, their strengths and areas of development, the signals about the system, etc. It is your genuine interest and curiosity about your team, instead of your curiosity about the issue, that lifts them from the dance floor and raises them to the balcony.

4: Be comfortable with silence

Many people are not comfortable with silence. In conversations, they feel that they have to say something in order to feel that they are contributing. As a leader, it is good for you to get comfortable with silence. You may want to acknowledge that it is an important way to be with someone. What's more important, creating a moment of stillness in conversations gives your team a chance to step up on the balcony, think clearly, and identify meaningful actions. It is difficult for them to access a balcony view if you struggle with the urge to fill the silence in the conversation.

So, next time you prepare for a coaching conversation or any other significant conversation with your team, do four things:

- Write down your intention on a piece of paper, next to meeting objectives and agenda
- During the conversation, treat what you are hearing as a signal from the whole system, focus on the person rather than the issue
- When it feels right, ask an honest, open question to support exploration
- Remember that there is great value in silence

These four steps will build your capacity to get your team on the balcony when it is most valuable.

Building deeper trust, faster

Tor Mesoy, Hong Kong

"For it is mutual trust, even more than mutual interest, that holds human associations together." – H.L. Mencken

A critical currency for leaders is trust. To lead effectively, we need to build and nurture trust with partners, subordinates, colleagues, clients, superiors, boards and other stakeholders. In a world that is becoming more integrated and where constellations often change rapidly, our ability to build deeper trust, faster, is critical to our securing impact and creating value.

In many of the leadership development programs I run, participants share with me that they are comfortable about building trust over an extended period – when they have months or years at their disposal, but they struggle to establish deep trust, rapidly. We don't always have the luxury of ample time so the question of how to build deep trust rapidly is an important one.

And it is possible. Let me give an example.

A few years ago, I worked on an international project with participants based in Scandinavia, the Middle East and East Asia. The constellation was brought together rapidly to design and produce a complex document that required skills in many different domains. The ten participants on our team belonged to six different organizations. They were hand-picked based on their expertise in the required domains – but many of us had never met, let alone collaborated in any way. We had two weeks to get to know one another, establish trust, agree rules of engagement, clarify roles and responsibilities, design our document, produce it and deliver it. The collaboration was exciting. It can be energizing to work with a new team, but none of us knew how this group of people would end up working together.

After addressing some initial confusion the team turned out to be productive. I felt confident that we would succeed when I observed one team member (let us call him Nils) express his opinion of another team member (let us call him Mo Pien): "I trust this man almost blindly." That is, of course, a strong statement. But it is particularly strong given that Nils and Mo Pien had never met, came from different countries, lived in very different places (Middle East and East Asia), and had different backgrounds. (It was years later that Nils and Mo Pien met, physically, and deepened their trust further).

As I reflect on how this team built trust in under a week, using only phone and e-mail, it struck me how four factors contributed. Team members demonstrated:

1: Credibility
2: Reliability
3: Intimacy
4: Low self-orientation

Credibility: Each team member brought their unique expertise to the table and made the choice to use it. They proactively shared ideas. They advocated forcefully when they felt strongly about a point. They asked insightful questions and challenged groupthink.

Reliability: The team members delivered their contributions on time. They performed reviews on time and they pulled no punches when they gave comments. They offered incisive, respectful critique, predictably.

Intimacy: The team members shared, appropriately, what was going on in their lives, and how this affected the time they had available and how they could contribute. Just as importantly, they demonstrated an ability to see the world from the angle of other team members. For example, when a team member did not meet expectations and was challenged, he or she would acknowledge that it was understandable that another team member felt let down - even frustrated. They would then proceed to rectify the situation to make sure they delivered.

Self-orientation: Each team member made it clear, through words and actions, that they focused on success for the client and the team, rather than on personal glory. People were helpful to one another and went out of their way to support others.

In the book *The Trusted Advisor*, Maister, Green and Galford bring together these factors in a catchy mnemonic – the trust equation.

$$\text{Trust} = \frac{\text{Credibility} + \text{Reliability} + \text{Intimacy}}{\text{Self-orientation}}$$

Many of us have one or two elements with which we are more comfortable. We may for example excel in the areas of credibility and reliability. In order to build deeper trust, faster, we need to fire on all cylinders. When we do this consciously, with authenticity and integrity, it is not Machiavellian. It is a worthy effort to make the world around us a better place. We know that teams with high levels of trust perform better. And at the macro level, we know that the economy of high-trust cultures tends to thrive; there is simply less need to validate and verify all the time. By observing others who have distinctive strengths, we can learn to fire on more cylinders. For example, the person who is strong on credibility and reliability may choose to open up and share a little more from the personal sphere. Or they may choose to make their intent explicit at the start of a meeting, making it clear that they are working in the interest of the other party.

As I have coached and mentored thousands of leaders over preceding decades, I have seen them strengthen their ability to build deeper trust, faster. It is well worth the effort

A powerful 4-step process for
giving feedback ...

Start with
observations/facts

2. Share
impact/feelings

3. Pause for
reaction

4. Offer actionable
suggestions

Giving feedback well to improve collaboration

Yan Liu, Hong Kong

Ten years ago, I was a function head in a fast-growing start-up. I was passionate about the work, but I had a difficult time with my boss. Regularly, what he did or said would make me feel confused, belittled, angry... and sleepless. Here are two examples:

- He asked me to lead a meeting discussing the goals of my function. At the start of the meeting, I suggested an agenda. He said that the focus was wrong, offered a completely different agenda, and took over the whole meeting. That made me look bad in front of my team. I did not understand why he did that. I wondered what I had missed in the process. I also wondered if he simply did not like me and actually wanted to make me look bad in front of others

- The company was preparing for a very important conference. I was requested at short notice to work with an external designer to design the flyer for the conference. I poured my heart (and a few nights) into the work to knock out a version that I was proud of. I showed him the design and asked for his input, hoping that he would say some nice words. He looked at it, frowned, and simply told me points that I had missed. After the exchange, I felt that my effort had not been acknowledged. I was disheartened, and rather angry

I worked with this boss closely for half a year. There were hundreds of such interactions. But I did not know how to speak with him. I kept thinking about why, and what I might have missed. I could only turn to family and friends for understanding and comfort. After the collaboration ended, I continued to wonder what I could have done differently in many of the tough and uncomfortable moments, how I could have communicated differently with this person to make my life easier and improve the collaboration.

Fast track a few years forward. I needed to facilitate a 2-day workshop for a group of 20 senior leaders including key members of the C-suite, as part of a year-long leadership development program for a client in China. It was an important workshop and the stakes were high. I had a fellow facilitator, Jane, with whom I was working for the first time. I had prior experience working with the client so I gave a lot of input on how she could run her sessions and what topics were most relevant to the group. In one session, she asked participants to form small groups and discuss questions which she said would be critical for the group. The CEO commented: "We have covered these questions with Yan and her colleagues before. I do not think they are relevant anymore." That gave her a hard time. She looked at me in passing and I could see that she was taken aback and confused. While she managed to continue the session, it went poorly. During the break, Jane came to me saying: "Yan, you said that those questions would be meaningful questions for this group to discuss, but clearly they were not. I wish you had told me this before the workshop." I told her that we would pick this up at the end of the day when we would have more time. When the day ended, we sat down, and had the following conversation:

Me: "Jane, I value our collaboration, so I want to be open with you regarding how I feel about our interactions. I believe open communication will help us build trust, do well in this project and continue the collaboration in the future."

Jane nodded.

Me: "You told me during the break: 'Yan, you said that those questions would be meaningful questions for this group to discuss, but clearly they were not. I wish you had told me this before the workshop.' When you said that, you spoke very fast and had a frown on your forehead. I sensed that you were confused and a bit angry."

I paused to allow her to respond, and she nodded again in acknowledgement without saying anything.

Me: "What you said made me feel accused and not trusted. As we prepared for the workshop, I wanted to tell you everything I knew so that we could deliver a successful workshop together. I do not know why the CEO said what he said, but it is incorrect.

He has never covered those questions with me. Maybe he had covered the same topic with another person, but I have no information about that. Next time something like this arises, I suggest that you ask me first, so that we can explore the reasons together, instead of you reaching a conclusion yourself without seeking my perspective."

Jane: "Hmm... you are right. It will be better that I suspend judgment, remain open, and discuss with you first. I jumped to a conclusion too quickly and what I said to you was unfair. I'm sorry for saying that and for making you feel bad."

We were then able to explore the situation together, and jointly decide on a way to follow up with the CEO. The workshop ended well. Jane and I had established deeper trust between us through the open communication and through our collaboration.

Giving one another feedback is an important part of a collaboration. Feedback done poorly, including not expressing feedback directly and in a timely manner, leads to confusion, anger, lower trust, conflict, and unsuccessful collaboration – like what I experienced with my boss in the start-up. If I had been able to share my experience of the interactions, to understand why he was doing things in certain ways, and to offer specific suggestions, we would have had a much better chance to understand each other's needs and adjust the way we interacted. I would certainly have spent less time thinking hard on my own, feeling bad, and not knowing what to do. However, the combination of my fear and lack of skills kept me from giving honest and constructive feedback to this boss.

What I did with Jane was to give feedback in a way that is well-intentioned, fact-based, timely and constructive. The five-minute conversation we had on the same day ensured that we understood the impact of the interaction, what I needed from her, and how we might work better together going forward.

What I did follows a simple and powerful four-step structure to give feedback effectively:

> 1: Observation - I noticed that you did/said...
> 2: Effect on me - What you did/said had this impact... / It made someone feel...
> 3: Pause for reaction - Do you know what I mean? Does this make sense? (or simply receptive silence)
> 4: Suggestion - Next time, I suggest that you/we try ...

While this may seem straightforward, it is often hard to give honest and constructive feedback in workplaces. Many things can get in the way. For example:

- Insufficient clarity on our intentions – we may think we are setting out to help the other, but if part of our intention is to vent anger or frustration, we are likely to meet resistance
- Insufficient discipline and skills to share concrete observations and having the habit of generalizing or coming across as judgmental – e.g. by saying "You always..." or – better, but still not great – "You tend to ..."
- Fear of hurting the relationship, so we choose to be vague in order to maintain superficial harmony, while maybe holding a grudge for a long time

Let me start by sharing with two practices that help create a positive context for such conversations:

- State the intention at the start of the conversation, sharing the benefit for both you and the other person if this conversation goes well. This helps establish a clear and joint purpose for the conversation and avoids the other person guessing your motivation – perhaps incorrectly
- Choose the timing well. As a rule of thumb, I recommend having the conversation sooner rather than later. This allows the people involved to learn from the situation and come up with solutions in a timely manner, without letting bad feelings simmer and have a negative impact on the relationship longer than necessary. But you may also need to adjust depending on the situation. For example, in relatively simple situations, and for teams that are used to having open communication, it is useful to give feedback right after the interaction. This allows the team to glean learning from a situation in a most timely manner and move on. In complicated situations, however, especially situations where the emotions are high, it is useful to give the people involved the time they need to calm down, and digest before speaking. Waiting for a day or two is typically enough

Here are the things you need to pay attention to when following the four steps of giving feedback, described above:

- While sharing observation, it is important to share facts only: what was visible in action and what was said. Avoid analyzing or interpreting the situation. Doing so will easily lead to a discussion of different analyses or even an argument about different interpretations
- While sharing the effect on you, it is critical to own the impact

by sharing your feelings. Your feelings are yours. Different people may have different feelings in the same situation, but it is hard to disagree with your statement about your own feelings. Sharing your feelings therefore tends to be met with acceptance. You may also share how the person's action may have affected a third person. For example: "I don't know if you noticed, but it was clear to me that she was furious. Her face went red and she fell silent. She stopped participating."

- It is critical to pause and check in with the other person that what you said makes sense and that they are following you. This helps avoid misunderstanding early in the process. Another reason for the pause is that it gives the receiver the opportunity to say something like: "I know what you mean. I have been working on this for some time. I struggle to behave the way I want to". This means that the door is open, and you don't need to knock. This affects how you perform step 4

- End the conversation with a concrete suggestion for what the other person can do, or what you can do together to improve the collaboration in similar situations

Honing our own skills in giving feedback in this way will be a blessing for those around us. And as awareness rises, we have a chance to build a true feedback culture where feedback is perceived as a gift and people are generous with these gifts, and they actively seek feedback for themselves. This creates a virtuous circle that rapidly deepens trust and raises performance. Every team can flourish at a higher level if the feedback culture takes root.

Chapter 4
Leading in an organization

" A leader is someone who holds her- or
himself accountable for finding the
potential in people and processes."

— Brené Brown

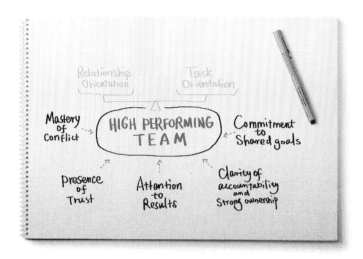

Building a high-performing team together
... as a team

Yan Liu, Hong Kong

Being a team leader and building a high-performing team is hard work. More often than not, you are faced with a number of challenges. Some team members are likely to disagree with you. There may be tensions among team members and the team atmosphere can be tense. When you need people to give their best, they may put in the minimum. People may seem busy but you don't see results. It is hard to assign new responsibilities. And often, trouble does not travel alone and you face many of these issues at the same time. You may well be asking: Where should I start? Who can help? One answer is: don't do it yourself, get your team to help you tackle the challenges of teamwork together. In this article I will share with you a story of how one team leader did it.

I recently worked with Max, a department head in a public institution in China. He took over a department of 30 people six months ago. In the process, he found many challenges as he tried to understand the team, and influence and shape it in a way that he deemed to represent an effective team. He was facing a number of challenges.

- He wanted to focus on getting things done quickly with high quality, but he often received pushback on timeline, scope, the value of a task/project, etc.
- As a result of such interactions, he ended up pushing people harder, micro-managing a lot, which, in turn, led to complaints from many team members
- He perceived that some team members thought that he had been pushing them because he wanted to impress his boss, and this harmed trust
- He pondered the idea of speaking with some team members to better understand the situation of the team and potentially even get their input or help, but he was concerned that they might perceive him to be weak and incapable if he did this

The list goes on.

It seemed to him that there were too many issues and challenges, and many of the issues were interconnected. For example, he needed the trust of some core team members to be able to speak with them openly and ask for their input, but he did not think the trust was deep enough for these people to give honest and helpful input. At the same time, without their input and support, it would be difficult for him to try any initiative to build a stronger team. He felt stuck.

Through a coaching conversation, he identified his goals, what was getting in his way, and the support he needed to start taking meaningful actions. His goal was to build a team that was open and trusting, and that could produce excellent results. His hesitation and fear came from worrying that he might be judged by the team as incapable, and being afraid of conflicts with the team members. He also identified the support he needed, namely an external facilitator to guide him and the team through an open exploration so that the team could understand the issues together, and work together to decide how to tackle challenges and improve teamwork.

Before working on improving teamwork, it is critical to understand what leads to high-performing teams. High-performing teams achieve great results while maintaining deep relationships with one another. Robert (Bob) Anderson and William (Bill) Adams shared in *Mastering Leadership* that the balance between task orientation and relationship orientation is a powerful indicator of leadership effectiveness. Effective leaders and teams strike a healthy balance between executing tasks and establishing relationships. As he explains in his book *Five Dysfunctions of a Team*, Patrick Lencioni found through his work with hundreds of senior teams that most teams encounter five dysfunctions at different stages on both task and relationship-oriented elements. These dysfunctions include: Absence of trust, Fear of conflict, Lack of commitment, Avoidance of accountability, and Inattention to results. These five areas cover the most important aspects of teamwork in terms of both task and relationship.

I worked with Max and designed a 2.5-hour workshop to have the team bootstrap their own performance. First they would reflect on and assess how well they were balancing their task orientation and their relationship orientation. Second, they would consider how well they were addressing the five dysfunctions. Third, they would put in place five key success factors to enable high performance of their team:

1: Presence of trust: team members have trust in one another's capability and motivation and they are willing to be vulnerable within the team to share personal limitations and challenges

2: Mastery of conflict: they embrace conflicts and have the mechanisms and skills required to deal with conflicts effectively

3: Commitment to shared goals: they have clarity of the team's goals and are personally committed to achieving these goals

4: Clarity of accountability and strong ownership: they set clear roles and accountabilities; they have a culture of calling out peers on counterproductive behavior and holding one another accountable

5: Strong results orientation: they always work with a clear end in mind; they have the habit of defining clear final outcomes before engaging in activities

Max and five of the team leaders in his department attended the workshop. Each person was asked to identify two areas where they believed the team was already strong, and two areas where they believed the team most needed to improve. Each person shared the thinking behind their choices:

- What made you think that the team was strong in that area?
  How could you as a team continue to build on this strength?
- Why do you believe it is critical for the group to strengthen an
  area? What is the consequence if you do not do that?

The picture below shows the group's self-assessment:

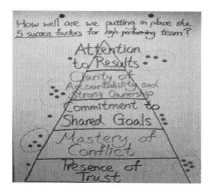

They identified two main strengths of the team:

- They were not afraid of raising different points of views, or
  even push back on leaders' requests mainly because the
  former department head had encouraged them to do that. At
  the same time, a few of them acknowledged that sometimes
  they could be more constructive in the way they raised
  different views
- They already had a strong habit of ensuring clear accountabilities, and most of the time, they had strong ownership of their
  responsibilities

They saw two areas where the group needed to urgently work to improve team dynamics:

- The level of trust was low, mainly because a) they had a packed schedule with little time to build personal relationships, and b) the leadership change half a year ago made them feel uncertain and they felt they still knew little about the new department head
- They did not have strong attention to final outcomes, because they were confused about the targets of the department, and what the department head wanted to achieve personally

This was a revealing process for the group. They said: "As a team, we are clearly strongly task-oriented and we have ignored the relationship part for a long time." Some said: "I kind of knew our problems, but it was such a strong confirmation to see the group's results come out in front of my eyes on a piece of paper." The department head found it most useful to know that the team was confused about his motivation, and the targets of the department, as he thought he had already shared these many times.

They then moved on to discuss how they might go about addressing the dysfunctions as a group, and what they personally would commit to. The whole group agreed that they would start to have casual lunches/dinners every month to get to know one another more deeply. Here are a few examples of personal commitments ...

- "I will share the vision, targets and priorities of the department for this year with the team and gain the team's understanding and strong support. I will do that in our team meeting next week." – The department head
- "I will show vulnerability by asking more questions and telling you where I need support; I will reduce micro-managing,

rather I will share with you the result I want and the standard of quality I expect, without dictating how you should do it" – The department head

- "I will continue to raise different points of views, but I will also propose suggestions and solutions instead of complaining or simply sharing opinions" – One participant

When I debriefed the workshop with the department head, he shared his biggest take-away: he realized that it took a team to build a team, and he couldn't do it himself. Through the workshop, he could get the core team to understand together their strengths, and the dysfunctions they needed to address. He now felt the onus was not only on him and he had the whole team working towards a common goal.

And he said it well. From my experience of working with many teams and team leaders, it is critical that the team leader creates a mechanism where the team can openly discuss issues, understand the importance of issues, and work together to resolve them collectively. Sitting down together to assess your teamwork in terms of task vs. relationship orientation, and the five success factors is a powerful way to tackle teamwork challenges and build high performing teams together - as a team.

Escaping the terror regime of meetings

Tor Mesoy, Hong Kong

The other day I met with a senior executive towards the end of the day. She looked haggard and gray in the face, low on energy and – frankly – somewhat desperate. She wailed: "I have been in meetings all day, back to back. It is a nightmare. I am not getting anything done!"

I empathized with her, but this was clearly not a great start to our meeting. She was deep in "victim territory," suffering from all those colleagues who were calling her to meetings. Of course, she was voting with her feet, and in some ways reinforcing the culture of exaggerated meeting activity by choosing to attend those meetings. Most of her colleagues were in the same situation – attending meetings as victims of too many invitations, and "not getting anything done".

This environment is not unique. Many of us recognize the situation. In fact, The Economist recently proposed Bartleby's Law: "80% of the time of 80% of the people in meetings is wasted."

But this particular encounter with this senior executive got me thinking: Why so much suffering?, What triggers such dysfunctional behavior?, What would it take to restore joy, energy and productivity? What requires attention here – the outer game or the inner game?

There are well-known remedies for making individual meetings more effective:

- Clear purpose, clear agenda
- Clarity around the objective of each agenda item: is it to disseminate information or to gather information or to make a decision?
- Clear invitation with unambiguous specification of the preparation work required
- Clear meeting process to ensure the right voices are heard and the agreed objective is reached in a timely and disciplined manner
- Clear actions agreed at the end, with specification of targets dates and responsible people

These are well known ... and they do make the individual meeting more productive. The techniques are easy to learn. They address the outer game – the observable behaviors. But they are clearly not

sufficient. Something deeper and more insidious is going on here –
something that cannot be addressed simply by adopting good
practices for designing and conducting meetings.

As I pondered the situation, it struck me that what is killing productivity on the altar of meetings is fear. Some of you may object to this
word. If you do, you can substitute "anxiety" or "concern" or "insecurity" or something similar. But these are simply various forms of fear,
and I shall use the word fear.

People calling meetings are, unfortunately, sometimes driven by of
one of three types of fear:

1: The fear of not being liked, of not having a sufficient sense of belonging

This fear can lead us to call meetings to ensure that everyone buys
into our decisions – beyond the level that is productive. Sometimes
the right course of action is to take an unpopular decision, stand for
something controversial and take the consequences – individually –
and accept that some people will not like this. It is simply not appropriate to seek everyone's buy-in for every decision. The downside is
too great. It takes too long.

2: The fear of not being seen to be smart or competent

This fear can lead us to call meetings where we demonstrate our
brilliance, perhaps by criticizing others and their work. Sometimes the
appropriate approach is to not blow our horn in public, but to have a
quiet one-on-one conversation to guide and support and nurture.

3: The fear of not being seen to be in control

This fear can lead us to call meetings to make sure that we are fully informed – of everything – well beyond the level that is productive. Staying informed is good, but there is a place for letting go and for trusting others. Sometimes it is appropriate to manage or lead by exception. Let people get on with it – without meetings – until an exception occurs.

The people attending meetings are, of course, also an integral part of the problem. They may be driven by similar fears.

- **The fear of not being liked** can drive us to attend meetings where we have little to contribute, mainly to engage in social grooming. In particular, we may feel the need to be "seen" at the meeting and we may want to avoid offending the person who has invited us. Attending fills a social function, but it hardly contributes toward meeting the objectives and the goals of the organization

- **The fear of not being seen to be smart or competent** can drive us to attend meetings and make sure we share our perspective at every turn, so that people see how good we are and how much we know. This is rarely the stated purpose of the meeting

- **The fear of not being seen to be in control** can drive us to attend meetings so that we know everything that is going on and what everyone is thinking. That gives us a semblance of control, but at high cost. It may be better to get on with 'real work' and catch up, as needed, when needed

As I have observed other leaders who "have so little time", who take work home on the weekend, who complain about running from meeting to meeting, who are uninspiring because they are drained and low on energy, I have become convinced that a culture of fear often induces this sad situation. In that context, adopting sound practices for the individual meeting is a band-aid. It can stanch the bleeding, but does not address the root cause.

What is required is deep personal reflection, with courage, so that we name and confront the fears that are affecting us, personally. This can take place in a group, but it is a personal journey. Assessment tools can help us, but they only hold up the mirror. What we do with the image we see in the mirror is our choice.

Together with my colleagues, I am privileged to run regular work-shops where we create a safe space for people to explore and name and confront their fears. When done courageously, it is tremendously liberating. It is transformational. There is no going back. And when we help one another, in our work environments, to perform this inner work, we empower people around us to become a lot more produc-tive. And happy. And fulfilled. This is deeply meaningful work.

So, consider the meeting culture in the environment where you work. How healthy is it? What gets in the way of it being (even) more productive? Is it sufficient to focus on the outer game (e.g. sound practices for running meetings)? Or is there a need to work on the inner game (e.g. confronting and overcoming fears)?

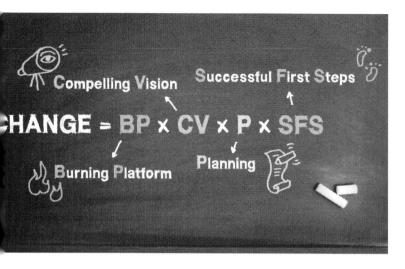

Using the Change Equation to accelerate positive change

Tor Mesoy, Hong Kong

I recently worked with a client in a declining market. The atmosphere in the company was rather glum. It seemed like most people had decided that there was not much that could be done about the structural forces buffeting the company, and the leaders were reconciled to navigating a genteel decline. Isolated voices called out for greater creativity and more entrepreneurship, but these were voices in the wilderness; their encouragements and admonitions had limited impact.

There actually *were* exciting opportunities to pursue, but risk aversion was high. In addition, there was a consensus that the market was against the company and that there was not much that could be done about this. Declining revenue did not constitute a burning platform. Rather, it was explained away. Several leaders had attempted to change this situation, but the effect had been limited.

In situations like this, creative thinking on how to make change happen – and stick – is required. There are many valuable models, theories and books that can support such thinking. Three favorite books of mine in this domain are:

1: *Switch* by Chip and Dan Heath
2: *Theory U* by Otto Scharmer
3: *Centered Leadership* by Joanna Barsh

These books present rich frameworks together with inspiring examples that can make change easier when it seems really hard.

In this article, I will share a simple framework that can be conveyed in minutes and that can serve as a useful checklist when change seems daunting. It is the change equation. It states that

CHANGE = BP x CV x P x SFS

Here BP is the burning platform, CV is the compelling vision, P is the plan and SFS is a series of successful first steps. Let me explain:

BP: The burning platform is critical. People must have a strong, personal feeling that the status quo is unacceptable. They must have the energy and the conviction to combat lethargy in themselves and in the people they lead. This can sometimes be achieved by modelling what will happen in the "do nothing" scenario. We can add fuel to the fire by encouraging people to confront truths that are often not discussed because they are too uncomfortable.

CV: The compelling vision is also key. And again, the vision for the change must be understood and embraced by the majority of people involved. Agreement is not sufficient. Ardent desire to see the vision achieved is required. This requires the vision to be specific, realistic (though it can be a stretch) and painted in vibrant colors. It must involve the intellect and the emotions of people. The vision work is not done until people go home and share the vision, enthusiastically, with friends and family.

P: A burning platform that is well understood and a compelling vision that is fully embraced are, however, not sufficient. I may grasp both of these but feel daunted by the journey. "It's all so big and complex. I don't know that I can scale a mountain that high". A credible plan is required. Often it does not have to be very detailed at the beginning. But it must be detailed enough to give confidence that we can execute each step and that the steps together add up to the required change journey.

SFS: Even if I have a good plan, I may waver. Others might be able to follow such a plan, but do I have the resources, the knowledge, the determination, the strength to follow this plan? Change agents may benefit from engineering small successful steps at the start of the journey and celebrate these successes with much fanfare. When I have successfully taken the first steps and can convince myself that the plan really only calls for more such steps, I strengthen my conviction that this is doable and I bolster my commitment.

I have often seen change achieved with spectacular success when these four factors were in place.

On the other hand, when change seems impossible or when change fails, one of these factors is typically missing or is too weak.

So, there you have it, a simple framework that you can use as a checklist and a diagnostics tool. Which factor, among the four, represents the weakest link in the chain in your context? How can you jointly get creative about ways to strengthen this factor? By listening deeply to the people involved in the change and by pooling your capacity for innovation, you will greatly increase our capacity for change.

Ground rules:
· Be candid, frank and ope
· No blaming of individuals
· Stay curious
· Listen deeply
· Offer your insights genero

1st case: a simple practice c
2nd case: a case that really i

An admirable example of a learning organization

Tor Mesoy, Singapore

"If we can really understand the problem, the answer will come out of it, because the answer is not separate from the problem."
— Jiddu Krishnamurti

What does it mean to be a "learning organization"? A lot has been written about this, with varying levels of insight.

Recently I was inspired by the executive team of a high-tech company that I work with. This team was determined to strengthen the learning capabilities of their organization, and they were taking concrete steps to speed up the learning and deepen the learning – both for themselves and the broader organization. This executive team was serious.

This drive for change was initiated by a real business challenge. The company had recently lost two large sales that had seemed promising. The sales team had worked for more than a year to lock in the new contracts and had received much encouraging feedback from the prospective customers along the way. And then – two painful losses in rapid succession. It would be easy in such a situation to become despondent or to focus on attributing blame. Instead, this team invited me to work with them to address three important questions:

1: What must we learn from these painful experiences?
2: How might we have gained this learning faster and at lower expense?
3: What must we do to ensure that in the future, we gain this kind of learning faster and less expensively?

We worked through a "5 x Why" analysis for the losses, moving down, level by level, from proximate to ultimate causes. For each level of the analysis, the team harvested insight and learning. And for each level they identified appropriate adjustments to strengthen the organization and its processes. But the impressive and inspiring part was the next step. The team asked: "How could we have gained this insight in an easier way?" and "How can we ensure that we do gather this kind of insight faster and more smoothly in the future – systematically?" In other words: "How do we accelerate and institutionalize learning in our organization?" These questions stimulated the team and helped them generate a rich set of next steps. We filled several whiteboards with insights and actions.

The global economy is suffering from a marked slowdown in productivity growth. If more leadership teams asked these kinds of questions when they encounter setbacks, much of the productivity challenge would be solved. I commend the courageous executive team that turned painful experiences into valuable learning opportunities.

Building leadership at scale

Tor Mesoy, Hong Kong

Many large organizations struggle to build leadership capacity at scale. It is an interesting challenge to achieve top team alignment and enhance the leadership capacity of the top team. Compared with this, it can be a daunting quest to build leadership capacity at scale: ensuring that the majority of people in the organization feel inspired, authorized and equipped to act as leaders. Yet, leadership at scale is increasingly required. The top team simply does not have the capacity to absorb and respond to all the signals that are reaching the organization. Messages get diluted and blurred on the way to the top, and responses from the top are too often slow or inappropriate. In many organizations it is critical to empower front-line people to respond effectively to opportunities: eliminate waste, streamline, simplify, meet new needs, experiment to learn rapidly, and respond effectively to external and internal change.

Why is this so daunting? In traditional, hierarchical organizations, we regularly observe a painful lock-in. Senior management feels it is their duty to be in control, or at least to be seen to be in control. They struggle to let go and to unleash creativity at lower levels. In such organizations, people lower down in the hierarchy have generally been conditioned to please their superiors and to comply with instructions. Challenges from below are often unwelcome by the top, and people have learned that nothing good comes from rocking the boat. If junior people challenge the status quo, they risk being censured. The focus is therefore on maintaining harmony. This combination of senior people projecting control and junior people seeking to comply easily results in stasis.

The tragedy of this situation is the lock-in. If change is driven from the top, subordinates resist, as they are fearful of the new messages that urge them to act in new ways that go against their mindset of complying. If lower or middle management attempts to drive change, senior management will resist, as the challenges from lower down are seen to undermine the authority of senior people; the senior people are concerned that they will not seem to be in control if they accept the new challenges from below. This lock-in helps explain why two thirds of transformation efforts fail.

It takes both patience and skill to overcome the lock-in, and it requires interventions at multiple levels.

It is necessary to work with the top team to nurture frankness, openness and vulnerability. The top team must, first of all, acknowledge that they have to change. They need to embrace the need to let go, accept risk in a controlled manner, and inspire, empower and enlist people further down in the hierarchy. This is threatening. It challenges the status quo. It therefore requires courage from senior management to choose this path. But for complex, adaptive change, it is the only possible route.

It is also necessary to develop leadership at scale, typically reaching thousands of more junior leaders to instill courage, grow the capacity to manage conflict, enhance communication skills, deepen problem solving skills and nurture innovation capacity. The only plausible way to do this is by leveraging technology. Webcasts and e-learning can contribute to achieving the required reach, but isolated technology pushes tends to have a fleeting effect, and people easily get jaded and cynical when they observe that the impact is limited. They become increasingly immune to the next push. To draw effectively on the technology, a level of social engineering is required: forming teams of people that support one another. Making sure that new information received is translated into personal commitments and followed up until people build new habits and the new way of working becomes natural. One environment that is promising in this regard is Potentialife (https://potentialife.com). It combines little snippets of directly applicable new information, life logging to track impact over time, nudges to engage in small, personal experiments, and support groups to ensure the experiments are carried out and that true learning is gleaned from the experiments. From personal experience: it works. Engaging in the Potentialife journey rapidly raises the consciousness of all participants and nudges them to use their strengths, configure their life for better health, engage more deeply in their work, strengthen relationships and enhance their sense of purpose. Together, this contributes to greater productivity, higher job satisfaction and overall a deeper sense of happiness. Powerful!

Because the approach is designed from the very start to be scalable, it allows reaching tens of thousands of people in a limited time. This can be one of the keys to unlocking the stasis described above.

There is of course much more to driving transformation, but I am excited to have discovered one partial solution that I expect will deliver great value in the years to come.

About Agnus Consulting

Agnus Consulting serves clients globally on topics of strategy, leadership and enterprise transformation. We prize "servant leadership", as reflected in our name (Agnus is the Latin word for lamb, a traditional symbol of servant leadership). We collaborate closely with clients to grow leadership capacity to further the strategic goals of the organization and help the individual leader thrive.

Values-driven, we know that our success is the results of our clients' success. We perform our work from the vantage point of top management, with deep understanding of functional and sector characteristics. We seek to build trust-based relationships with our clients. Together, we strengthen sense of purpose, overcome the fears that get in the way, and unleash the potential of peak performance – both at the personal and at the collective level.

Who we are

Tor Mesoy is the founder and CEO of Agnus Consulting. His mission is to support senior leaders to be the best they can be, so they live fulfilling lives in keeping with their gifting and create sustainable, meaningful change in their organizations. A former partner of McKinsey and of Accenture, Tor has supported more than 4000 leaders on all continents through his coaching, teaching and counseling. Tor lives in Hong Kong.

Yan Liu is a leadership coach and facilitator in Agnus Consulting. She designs, delivers and manages organizational development programs. Her passion is to facilitate individuals and teams to become more effective at solving meaningful problems and creating positive impact in society. She is from Mainland China, and lives in Hong Kong with her family. She enjoys reading, swimming, and practicing Tai Chi.

Lucy Qian is a leadership facilitator and coach in Agnus Consulting. She supports leaders to deepen their self-awareness, unleash their potential, and achieve self-expansion. She feels most fulfilled when she coaches people to uncover self-limiting beliefs and adopt more liberating ones. She lives in Hong Kong with her family. She enjoys hiking, reading and cats.

Claire Wang is a talent development consultant, facilitator, and certified coach with Agnus Consulting. She works with organizations to design learning programs to develop their talent. She also supports individuals to reduce interferences and unleash their full potential. She is an amateur yoga practitioner, an anthropologist, and – always – a student.

Nick Chatrath is an Expert Advisor at Agnus Consulting. He is a coach, facilitator of transformation, entrepreneur and author. As a certified Master Executive Coach, Nick has over 2000 hours of 1:1 coaching. Nick chairs two boards and is writing a book about AI and human flourishing. Nick lives in Oxford with his wife and three daughters. He enjoys sprint triathlon and cooking.

Warren Ang is part of the extended team at Agnus Consulting as a leadership development coach, facilitator and trainer. He is a senior leader and practitioner in the global development and non-profit sector with a background in strategy consulting in both private and public sectors. He founded Global Development Incubator's East Asia presence and serves as its Managing Director. At GDI, Warren works with mission-driven businesses, foundations, governments and non-profits to design and build start-ups and initiatives that achieve large-scale social impact. Warren holds an MBA from INSEAD. Currently he lives in Hong Kong with his wife.

Tomas Gustafsson is an associate of Agnus Consulting, a seasoned facilitator, trainer and master coach. He has provided leadership development to more than 12,000 people from many types of organizations, ranging from SMEs to 54 Global Fortune 500 companies. He thrives on partnering with leaders in the journey of self-discovery and expanding consciousness. He has a profound passion to inspire people to embrace their potential through discovering and integrating their talents, strengths, experience and emotional drivers. He lives with his wife and their three creative children in Singapore.

Noel Sy-Quia is an associate of Agnus Consulting, a leadership development facilitator, master executive coach, and writer. Noel brings a balance of strategy formulation and implementation skills to his clients. In spanning strategic thinking, process definition and leadership development he helps client organizations align capabilities, practices and culture to long-term performance goals.Noel draws on over 20 years of business leadership experiences to facilitate complex problem-solving and high-performance collaborations across multiple business functions and national cultures. He lives in the United States.

Our team and events

Find out more

Web: www.agnusconsulting.hk
LinkedIn: Agnus Consulting
Email: contact@agnusconsulting.hk

Our approaches:
In our quest to deliver impact and value for our clients, we customize solutions to meet specific client needs. Here are some examples of how we work:

We help you understand where you are and who you are ...
- Personality assessments
- Self-exploration toolkit (e.g. personal values, strengths, vision, sources of meaning)
- Leadership style and competency assessments
- Team effectiveness assessments
- Leadership culture assessments
- Organizational diagnostics
- Specialized assessments (e.g. conflict management style)

We support your personal growth, transformation and leadership development ...
- Facilitated workshops
- Coaching
- Training (e.g. public speaking, powerful communication, problem solving, leading change)
- Learning lab: peer coaching processes for self-exploration and problem solving
- Labyrinth: a form of walking meditation for self-discovery
- Immersive experiential learning activities

- Technology-enabled learning and development solutions
- Wilderness trail
- Design and implementation of "corporate universities" and similar institutional capabilities to develop leaders

We work with you to solve real problems and develop your team and organization ...

- Shaping and leading transformations (e.g. agile, high-performance, enhanced customer orientation, greater innovation)
- Team alignment
- Team building
- Creating organizational vision, mission and values
- Strategy development
- Strategic projects
- Mediation and reconciliation

Printed in Great Britain
by Amazon